The Cloned Mammoth

THE CLONED MAMMOTH

Martin Reyto

Quadrant Editions

Copyright © Martin Reyto, 1981.

Published by Quadrant Editions, RR 1 Dunvegan, Ontario
K0C 1J0. Distributing c/o English Department, Concordia
University, 1455 de Maisonneuve Blvd. West, Montreal,
Quebec H3G 1M8.

Some of these poems have previously appeared in
Fiddlehead, *Matrix*, *Quarry*, *Prism International* and *The
Montreal Writers' Forum*.

Typeset in Bodoni Book by Trigraph (Toronto), printed and
bound by The Porcupine's Quill (Erin) in August of 1981.
The stock is Zephyr laid.

Cover is after an etching by Otto Graser.

ISBN 0-86495-009-8

for John Fraser

The Prisoner

what is poetry to a prisoner
is nothing to you: two minutes' tedium.
is commonplace to you. you're not there
when his body goes taut as a dying plant
sucking moisture from the night air.

the murderous device of silent prayer,
the fusion of the limbs into
mental contortions of divinity, are unknown
to you. the whole world watches the prisoner,
on a screen or through glass, when
he lifts his insect-arms together
and cries against the wall.

stranger than any dream. reports of
death, flagellation of a mythical weather,
sun that draws a man's heart
out of his side, a tethered dessication, and
a silence of death are hinted at. the papers lie.
their purposes meet in networks of somnolence.

there is no poetry for you. there are no
politics for you. no death for you.
the prisoner has no voice, and at the end
no light. enforced to something like human peace
he counts off the hours of a single night,
speaks one sentence to the wall and stares
until the words are written there.

the death of the meanest insect
is equivalent to a sunrise.

Hunted

the quick thrush feasts
in the bush of piety
the killed thrush rains glass
on the snow of reason

rises with
a tree's arms
experimental fingers
a caress of leaves: all this
will live a hundred times before

your hands
(old uncles staring into wells)
draw souls

your fingers catch
in the web of satiety
steeple in prayer over all
that could gladly die
but for dying

his dying
wings explode out of the frozen tree
and crash into the drum
of the hunter's lassitude

8

Schubert
and the White Field of January

Schubert wanders
in the field of January
a lost melody
in a thread of wind

defeated pain
gentle monotony

(I also wander
in this wide field
and stand still

Schubert sweeps the snow
around my feet
white dust

and trails the snow
across the wandering
bleak miles)

2.

should you too come
to the white field of January

should we meet, our
hands touch — should we kiss
and lie down

and love, and be born
to the stillness, the blue hills
the white hills

9

the pink and the gray
ribbons of cloud,
should we be
like the sky

mute,
translucent
and say, O

come sleep, come
let music wander
around and beneath us

3.

Schubert in still-life
at the piano: the flame of a candle
shines in each eye

4.

the music-bearing wind
leaves no footprint, only
small bent flowers

scattered and red
on the shifting white

10

Soldiers

one lives, one dies.
one finds a brown toad
to follow in his life
another is given
the oboe of mercy
the bells of solitude
and one leaves with no gift
to hunt golden deer.

one day they meet up again
past generations broken
across the ragman's cart
where hands and the food they grappled for
are frescoed in equilibrium.
now their own weight is gossip
exchanged by frightened crows:
this one followed the toad of mercy
this one the deer of solitude.

deep in the night when fortune
swells our sleep like new bread
at dawn when the still light
quickens with our children

they sit on the ground.
they bow to the wind
of unspeakable memory.
dogs bark the year round

Pig Song

you know, I
woke up yesterday with
a pig's nose, I was

a prime candidate for slaughter,
with a mind full of
streets, cars, wire and money.

desire becomes me
handsomely. desire
gnaws at my nerves

makes my legs
twitch

at night, in bed, when
I should be still,
then

comes this sordid electricity.
God
damn me if I'm crass with you.

12

it seems a little death hides
in the reality of anything
other than today, this hour

like an unmailed post card.
another year past,
my possessions begin to breathe
I've added their weight

to my weight. you know,
it is never, has never been
always like this

the streets littered with dusty coins —
for example now I am lean, with
a parakeet's head

I ride a motorbike on
the glass highway, down
the lean hours of night

I come to where you are.

13

Lullaby

I know the way
these muscles unclasp and send
a day's worth of anger scuttling like
spiders across the bed
I know the way of this body
its ease is not a happiness

and now red flowers
curl about the moon and hands
nudge the symphony of the world down
to rest. and the noise of
hungry murderers leaks
like water from a barrel, bleeds
silence

breaks out in the cracks of sleep
or in the tortuous guesswork of
a poem unfolds
many-petalled, in screens, mirrors
and now the hungry shout, they go
gawking in the street with mad eyes

the murderers, undoing
the fragile veils of night,
I wonder who they are.

14

Bottom of the Well

at the
bottom of the well
each day takes on
the aspect of a concave moon
morning noon and twilight

and night stares into the
well's mouth like a mirror
one is caught in or
an ink-filled balloon or
some ovoid complexity girdled
with a great swath of stars.

the well opens into weather
and weather opens into light
light opens into water
and water stares at the meals of night

with the majestic hunger of a reptile

15

'Murray Walters worked late'

wrote the machine
and then Murray went home
catching the last train
to Herridgetown
to the George Herridge farm
and Herridge's bed
where Murray lay down.

millisecs drone like helicopters down
the sky of centuries: ruminations flash
in the silicon synapses
that Murray will later
declaim from the platform
yes that's when his arms
are nailed to the arch and he
chirps like a saint while the walls sprout plankton.

'you're tired'
said the machine
and so I went home
and laid me down in Terrytoontown
sleep came easy
a salad doze
but never did I sleep so well as when
I photographed Murray from the console screen
drifting behind his glasses in
infinite recession.

16

Two Heads

after all the years
I carried his bud
nested in my heart

the bound tendrils
of his body shot out of my neck like
the last shaft of a bamboo tree

first I from our mother
then he from me.
I carried him around like an ape's child

I ate his food he slept my sleep
at public occasions I stood apart
in high-collared gowns preferring

to be merely hunchbacked
the joyous women didn't pass me by

and my brother's dreams
fed my vigil
with absolute fragility.

17

2.

who will give a headless man a job?

where the sky's skin is taut howling
plants drag their tumescent fruit
to the mating-place of crabs and I him

I will sever you with a dull stone
I will root you out
I will tear you into the world

like a sprouting tulip bulb
oh god so I might sprawl
and eat the silence of this gilly jell

then gone the truths and lies
between us
our wisdom always a moot point

having sucked life clean
the twelve teeth
in his false mouth chatter only

once in our existence
extracted from my thorax this carrot
this surgical wunderkind this root

cries out it's
dry here
DRY
DRY

Perfection

he admired her from afar:
wove her out in nets of admiration
until she was attenuated
into rays of her own colours, which were pure.

he hated every walking hour.
at the office, rows of desks became
grades of divinity, the spiral way
to where she sat.

he astonished himself daily.
on the subway, his eyelids concealed
murder, dismemberment, the
innocent hacked to pieces

for leading unfevered lives.
guilty of intervention, their sparse
heads split under hatchets
for daring, in life, to be stonelike.

there is no greater romantic than a murderer:
she gave him a weekend
and Monday morning first thing he marched
up to her desk and slapped her

down to the floor, a whore now no
different from the wood, fabric, concrete and glass
which encased them. perfection
came to him that suddenly. perfection consumed her.

As the Cosmic Egg

I was lost for centuries,
elephants played soccer, finding
my naked form forsaken
and rotund on the savannah

by that time I resembled a crystal ball
dropped by alien civilizations again
and again on the revolting grasses
by that time I'd consumed
entire cities
countries, continents
and still and still
you may pick me up in the palm of your hand,
I'll flower there

index poverty on this wracked skull
index meteorology:
lunatic budgie-snatchers
skulking around Woolworth's
with empty shoeboxes, eyeing the cages
wear me, wedged tight
between their brains and spines
under their coats I have sucked up
curious toddlers
their mothers

20

their nights, their beds, their houses,
oh the playgrounds and the
and the streetcars they took
to get from there to here and it is
and it is I who move their
dirty old hands to the cage door
make them
dip in
merge their
gray wrist-bones and gray hands
with a blue-green
chattering and tweeting universe: I
became
a crystal ball, aggressive reflector,
planted in a mountain I sucked up Pompeii
I filmed it over, inside out, it was
holocaust in reverse,

and my dreams were profuse
with antlers and children and holidays.

21

Ulysses

boasting that the test of wit
is the work he performs without hands
he sings for cats at the club's back door
dreams carpets of infamy.

in orange summer the earth inclines
to the sun and ladders rise
from the deserts of neighbouring worlds

his voice and the moon fill half the horizon

and the boarding of captives in the strange dawn . . .

fire shoots from his pockets as the lane
ejects him into the boulevard: rabid mice
whirl out of the cinders
against the crowd's teeth

he shrugs off the night like an
old coat, his heart
engorged by langorous tongues

whose singing has caught him at a hundred doors.

22

The bird-woman once knew how to pose for a mirror, but that is behind her now. This, were she aware of it, would be to her great advantage. There are women, men too for that matter, who muffle their bodies in layers of nylon, cotton, and tweed. Her hands like to knead their steaming pores, their white secret creases. Their odours sometimes catch her nose unawares, through any purchased scent, the desperately quiet exhalations of their clothes. These people grew up in winter, and they reproduce, proliferate, and die in much the same way. She can grab the untearable stuff in both hands and whirl men and women out of it like butterflies. Or swallows. But that is not exactly the point.

Once the bird-woman knew how, by tensing tiny muscles in her chin, to give her lips a clarity of definition others must accomplish cosmetically. Now she no longer has the time, in fact her whole face has acquired the formlessness of one lost in a highly exacting state of wonder: her mouth the shape of an O, painful to look at but inscrutable, and certainly beyond anyone's help if that were in the least relevant to her thoughts and activities. Our own imaginations offer us only the most tenuous survival.

She was taken with the lives of birds. In mid-June, when her Maserati revved and howled with freedom down curving Alpine roads, hitchikers in rain-capes loomed out of the clouds and flashed by her like wounded cranes. Flapping and hoarse cries disturbed her in the night, until she'd wake out of a windswept, glacial place to hot silence and a ticking alarm clock and hide her face in her hands to preserve, for a few more ticks of rediscovered time, that rocky land where the cliffs and crevices were mottled and fuzzy with down and bird-dung and the brittle air was thick with their suffering.

She was arrested by the police on a narrow ledge outside a fifteenth-storey office window in downtown Manhattan. This was last fall; the charge was corporate espionage. She protested in vain that a clothesline in Queens would have served her purpose just as well. It was a short extension of that very argument that put her in a prison cell. But then the war broke out and she, along with everyone else, was released to the furnace.

Today she hops up to me on the mosaic tiles of a new subway station and stares at my outstretched hand with one startled red eye, then with the other. She is dressed to look as inconspicuous as possible in the tired, midwinter commuter crowd. Round glasses, brown tweed coat, a pocket romance clutched in one tan-gloved hand. She talks to me about her new job, new friends, a recent lover. She is glad about the abundance of underground shopping malls in Montreal. Everything she needs to know is in the papers. She never feels caught short. When she stops talking, her mouth drops into the shape of an O. She no longer has any time. A tiny muscle in her cheek twitches, writhes, then lies still.

24

The Night Man

you, trapped in the cold, give
me your comfortless fingers, hide
your stinging face against me

I am the night man, large
as a tree, warm as the blood in your heart,
when winter comes for your secrets and
stands in the doorway with a burlap bag
I take you away to my bed, you
can sleep there

I am dark as the dark above the snow
I am at home when there's no one home
I am what you know when you don't know,
your old friend in every group of strangers,
a man of the night.

you, lost among footprints, too
many friends and too many walls, give
me your eyes and old dreams will flower there

I am the night man, strong
as the fist in your heart

when you are too busy I keep your memory
when you are tired I strike you blind
steal you from the useless races
even when you want to stay and try

I take you to death when you want to die
and wordlessly wait there.

Jenny Wren

It was a Jenny Wren dream
she was small with a large head
and the rest of her was motley, like
a quilted bird.

I caressed her ruffles in bed, she
looked at me with wide eyes:
you big ox, she said, to do this
as if you were in love.

I am, I said, it's just the strangeness,
the way your neck tapers into
such a fanciful thing, a tiny sweep
of feathers on the pillow, nothing more —

it takes — I'll get
used to it after a while.
and she: as if it weren't you I saw
carousing with the toy dog all afternoon.

yes it was true. but her child and I
chased the leaping stuffed terrier back
into the closet and I was weaving something
straight out of my hands, from nothing

I said 'what am I doing? it's
so strange' and the child came and hugged me
(the strangeness of it
had made me lonely)

whirl went my hands over each other
and out poured an endless stream
of golden yarn
and swirled down in a deep pile on the floor.

26

Lise

just before dawn
Lise walked out from among the trees
stepping softly on the wet stones,
naked and white.

the water rippled
and gurgled quietly.

2.

her skin rippled as the water slowly rose
with a reflection of stars.
she saw the stars around her
and now she knew
what was beneath them.
she slid her hand beneath them.

later on
mist covered the sunrise.
the lake turned the colour of mercury.

27

3.

Lise, a mad girl,
drowned herself, and her dog
found his way back to the house
toward mid-morning.
the goat grazed around the stone well.
the rooster blinked behind
its wire mesh
in the glaring, yellow sun.

Lise's father made the motor of the old truck
roar
and the hot white dust
rise and whirl in the yard.

4.

Lise's mother was too frightened to weep

the eyes looked more
mad than Lise's eyes

the colour of bright mercury.

28

Wildflowers

ladies with dead
hushands, wearing
clay-smeared bandannas
bow in the rain in lost fields,
put down their baskets.

the mortal way
their clothes turn yellow —

they sway in the moonlight, rake the
dust where horseflies shat their young,
pack the weeds with old
knuckles, gold rings.
and they
crinkle their eyes till the night
splits
and folds like a paper fan

they stare at the backs of their hands,
and roots tap
the bones in their calves.

29

She was taken apart bit by bit, without the horror of sudden
mutilation. Even at the age of twenty-five her beauty had
been of the kind which is itself nearly featureless, made
translucent by another beauty of overwhelmingly alien
configurations. It made her face difficult to remember from
one meeting to the next, and nearly unrecognizable in
photographs.

I know that early age makes this force seem benign: the
delicate awareness of one face beneath another, altering
the significance of a look, blurring the turn of the lips, a
game of lantern-light and molten glass in which everything
is tranquil and possible. But later, when her face revolted
and grew hard, love beat its way out of her with hammer
and chisel, depriving her even of the dignity granted to
animals. Before it was over, her magnificent hair was cut to
thistle, her torn limbs gaped in my sleep like milestones,
and the rooms of light in her eyes became diamond
drill-bits where desperate gnomes worked in her for
freedom at any price. One summer evening, as I sat
outside and watched her pedalling on her tricycle and
leaning out sideways like a badly used rag doll, I fell to
wondering: she was compelled, her need now past any
power of speech or comprehension, to drive that ridiculous
toy around and around on the lawn as frantically and
furiously as if the integrity of the universe depended on it.
I thought with a very bitter nostalgia that this was the only
way I had ever known her; but this had not always been the
way she was.

Heroes of the Metro

he reaches into
her tidy winter coat and takes
an armpit in each hand

his glasses glitter close, she sees
a funhouse of flawless lenses, bristle,
eyes, jaw, brown nose-holes. his compressed beak

targets her neck, sucking
surgically, as if on a fistula

there's nothing there
nothing there for you to eat
or cure

for her it's a case of nerves:
she dangles in his clutch and jerks
like a marionette tangled in a power line

I'll see you tonight

31

The Cloned Mammoth

my name is a clean, pure joke

I wear my alibi like a saint's cowl,
hum with spurious relief
the bee-song that makes its
excuses at nightfall.

they saw me again, wrinkled by weather,
churning snow with my feet while my head
rattled with drums. jabbered
with birds. spreadeagled in fern. while wind
whipped the music like a naked gypsy
their boots crunched past, a long
oration of bursting pomegranates.

oh christ, alone
another night to eye
the rat-turds of exile by a small lamp:
fear gnaws at the house. I turn
to where the wall opens into sleep and fall there
to old anatomies of nails and wire.

the thing that eats me is stronger
than the thing I feed on.

2.

I fear the garbage truck

and bits of coal in the yard.
and the thaw days

when the fence begins to crack and slide away,
when the neighbour's daughter unfurls
a string of huge underpants on the clothesline
and dogs in the alley straddle each other
with rolling eyes.
I have grown afraid of my books
and have lost at both sides of my chessboard

locked hand-to-hand with alien minds
I iron my shirts at two a.m., only one
in the morbid
sequence of their nightmares.

3.

my name is pure.
the planet attacked me

stretched against a fence in the white night
you slept through.
a rifle and a shadow
a door
open to death

I saw

its little eyes and the
welling time between its tusks, the frothing
millenia that spilled from it
like burst pomegranates, I blew out its
tiny brain with one shot

just because once I was human.

Marvellous the Pleasant Crab (a Novel)

THE PLEASANT CRAB.

the pleasant crab
walks in the shoes of
soldiers torn across the
rusty blade of war.

destruction alive
only in his genes, he dances
every day, as if time
were made especially for him,
to squander.

PAR LA MER.

down here by the sea
not much remains of your
D-day carnival.

nothing of the bones of men
sawed in half by war.

in an interesting still-life
we see little Marvellous, the
pleasant crab, ascend the beach

poised on horror's narrow brink
but grinning like a miniature
General Eisenhower,

the first and last ashore.

(EPILOGUE.)

you, overseer, pace along
time's sloping shoulder and
chatter like a parakeet.
you have seen all the slides
and insist that the case calls for an
autopsy. but the patient is still alive!
then a dissection, a dichotomy!
we must get out of this clean!
we must get to the bottom!
but he *is* at the bottom! Bah
Christ! how you perplex!
confounding everything!
then let him stay there!

CHAPTER ONE.

the pleasant crab
walks in the shoes of
soldiers torn across the
rusty blade of war.

he asks: who among us
saw it happen? and
dances a jig
kloppity-klop-klop in big boots,
backwards,

as death does.

New England

the hills are terse.
one day left in the year
and they've been cheated of snow.
here's another poet:
a shiver runs through the brass lamps,
a clock chimes ten. his parents' house.
there are too many rooms to heat.
upstairs, in the dark,
the ghost of his grandfather mutters under cold quilts
and tries to masturbate. the floor creaks.
then another clock chimes ten.
then another.

he snarls at such absurdity
but the fact remains, in this house
there are three of each o'clock.
no amount of precision will help here.
he dreams of setting a blowtorch to the carpets.
everyone dreams. he knows that.

36

he sits by the fire with his elbows on his thighs
and stares at the embers, the bricks, the grate.
everyone knows what he knows. he knows that.
but his knowledge of *that*
is what sets him apart
from the charlatan and the hack.
he gives his knuckles a loud crack.
he stares at the floor.

black hills gather on each other
and surround the house like hairy mothers
(it's a tense waiting for midwifery)
(cf. Wordsworth or Coleridge in something or other).
his wife is asleep and pregnant in the next town.
now his mother shuffles into the parlour
in detestable sleep attire. says,
James, why don't we ever talk any more?
we were so close once.

37

R.O.M.

at the Canadiana Gallery of the R.O.M.
you know it's spring because
the window is open in the men's room.

I opened it.

but in the office it's still February,
the secretary won't let me smoke & she
made me climb a ladder
to block off the air vents with tape
and cardboard. as if I'd
put those bloody air vents there.
passing the windows, she glowers,
their very capacity for being open annoys her.
of course they're shut tight.

so I make a quiet exit, armed
with tobacco and Vogue papers, to the men's room.
I bolt the door in the metal stall and
lean dreamily on the narrow sill,
watching green-headed pigeons
lead their stupid lives on a cornice.
gentlemen with clamouring bowels
burst in, then depart with
exasperated groans. let them go
shit in the broom closet. I conceive

sleepy, sunny revolution,
a beautiful tentacled beast who comes
with glittering eyes & a smell of come and seaweed
to squeeze these bricks till the whey runs out.

38

2.

I'm going to try
to rob this place blind.
I'm going to clean out
the storage cupboard. lay in
my *own* stock of paper clips,
erasers, letterhead, carbons, index cards.
friends will ask, amazed,
Where did you get it?
I'll say: I thank & God bless
the Canadiana Gallery of the R.O.M.

my poems and I
are part-time employees. we
lurk like castrated guerrillas
among the pottery shards, the dolls,
the antique chairs. in a half-dream
we hear our high-pitched sighs
drift down the stairwell
and we follow them with a steaming
mug of Nescafe at 10:00 a.m.

Wolfe on the Plains of Abraham clutches
at his fleeing blood & his eyes fill
with vision, the clanging, steel-belted
corridor to the future
and the Canadiana Gallery of the R.O.M.
peers back at him from the other end
tended all winter by ghostly rats: me,
stern-lipped female guardians of our
manners, our office supplies
our dominance and our wealth,
& various turkeys and weirdos, the scholars & gents.

Piano Lesson

I could never get along with average people
he says
sitting on a Sears catalogue kitchen chair
in a bachelor apartment
in a housing development
for senior citizens in a northern suburb
of Toronto, surrounded by four gas stations
a hamburger stand
and a brown expressway

I always wanted my freedom
he says
at the age of sixty-two
motherless fatherless womanless childless
(he says) I've lived only for my music
since the age of *five*.

he says: I teach two lovely children
every Wednesday evening
they have a lovely feeling for the piano
that expression which can't be *taught* you know
it can't be taught

40

and the first time I went there
their father (such a lovely man) said to me
'Mr. Green, you like soup?' and I says, why
sure I like soup and he says, 'well come and
have some soup with us, it's just ready,' he said. Well!
imagine me! eating with a family after all these years!
it felt very strange you know.
I felt very strange.
then the next week he says to me, 'would you
like to have some mushroom omelette?' and since then
they don't even ask me any more, it's become a habit:
after the lesson I simply go upstairs and sit down.
I tell them jokes you know: oh I cut up
something awful! I think they like a little humour.
I think that's why they have me.

as I grow older
he says
I find I've reached the point with my music
where I no longer have to worry about technique.
I've learned all I can ever learn.
I do not profit by listening to others
the amateurs, the average people.
I learn only from the greatest musicians
in the world. I learn from Mozart, Beethoven, Chopin.
yes I can jump right into the deep end of Beethoven
because I *experienced* it all. in my twenties

I had a very tragic experience.
I took a very long time to mature.
but I don't think a man can be an artist
till he's past forty, do you? in my thirties
I was in a very bad state of mind
for years. I would have gone for a psychiatric examination
today that would be simple enough
but in those days
it was something to keep secret, shameful you know
so I didn't go.
I opened up a book of songs by Schubert
you know how tranquil and peaceful they are
and I played them, I felt their peace invading me
and so I got over it.

(he adjusts his toupee,
too large for him, I note,
and smiles:) you see? my
music helped me through
the hardest times of my life. I think
that may be why
I am so attached to it.
to me no one is greater than Mozart.
so quick, so lively, so full of whim — that's me!
that's my kind of music!

42

(he's playing the piano: his feet
stretch for the pedals, his hands
strike chords, then fumble on the keys
the small fingers trip over each other
as his jaw grinds, lips writhe, head turns
to the ceiling
god knows what he's hearing

clusters of dissonance
tumble Chopin into nonsense
melody spreads its wings
and crashes into grumbling bass
where it is plucked, eaten, spat out in gobbets

my eyes trace the music
in the patterns on the rug
I am betraying him
my presence deprives him of everything
in this room where my limbs are too large
where the half-scale furniture shines with his vision;
and I, a Goliath of dead meat, nod and
smile my idiotic understanding smile
and can be no more than this for him, though he tries
so hard to tell me what he means
and seems so convinced
I'm his friend, and says to me:)

we see much more than average people see

43

Cricket

in late afternoon comes
the cricket's cry

and the molten sun
bronzing the still poplar leaves

now the beating and whirr of the wings
of a single bird rising
tips gilded in a white flash

then
the presence of the bird
lingers
at the centre of the rippling silence

then gone

2.

in the cricket's back
is a jewel, black as the night's eye
hollow, hard
against the damp ground

and the jewel of the cricket
shrills
as evening seeps into the sky
and the distant chirp expands
blending with the earth, the weeds, the
chill air, the iris and the
cooling stone

44

the inquiring monotone
of the cricket
remains

3.

black sky
alive with an intensity of stars
and a ghost of love

the sorrow eludes prayer

but in the vibrant formation of spheres
of light and the muted song of benevolence
returns a song of desire
the cricket's echo

45

Crow

resting, the crow lights
on one tree and the next
and so multiplies

but in flight he divides the sky
into two planes

as an expert draftsman might
with space and two lines
create sky

so the guided certainty
of crow-flight.

clouds dense
at the valley's rim

white splinter
of a dead pine

spring creek spreads like mercury
among the reeds
below the hills
and the mercury sky

46

where cry and silence meet
rain rests on separate leaves
a leaf tips rain to the grass
and beaded cobwebs weave
leaves to each other

in the vanishing recession
of these minute acts of love
among the countless, separate
spirits of the world, the crow
and the space around him
assume each other

cry

spring creek spreads like memory
among the reeds

rain drifts into mist
gradually amazed

47

The Fool

the actor in the film
was cast in the role of a fool.
hour after hour he lay in a sunny field
his hands upstretched and moulding
the absurdly distant sky.
some birds flew by.
the film was called
the Fool.
the hero lay on his back in a field.
a grasshopper crawled up the screen
in a bunch of queen anne's lace.
its space-helmet eyes
searched the audience.

one night in dead winter
I'll dream about The Fool:
a man sleeps in a sunny field
and his sleep dissolves
in a flight of silent blackbirds.
leaves and wildflowers begin to grow
at the corners of his eyes
and a grasshopper turns
on his loose, dry lips, and stares.

48

Madonna

the
girders
riveted sunk
solid and deep in the cracking
clay floor where the weeds of my absence
sprout curl wither crack dry
where pass the
soldiers clowns and chimpanzees
the candle procession of blind saints
where all things
sent and received by the eyes roll
by in bas-relief inciting
music impelling
it through abstraction forcing
speech
contact with
air the
physical irrevocable mechanical
THUMP as the pitiful proud hand
begins to move caress and curl
around and clutch this finally
graspable clay   your words

your words all
and if the hand's efficacy
the transmitted prayer
should move you to see me
erecting the iron
beams of despair
let the end of my work
like the pale scent of dew
in the unfelt violet air
at moonrise linger
around your hair

49

Psalm

horses heavy with hay
horses heavy with springwater
rocks glow and squat
like toads among mirages
the guide's hands uncurl
and crack across the palms
roads disperse where they
once merged

horses loaded
with dates and gourds of honey
lashed in the clear night
by the tail of the quarter-moon
asleep by heaven's gaslight
and fanned by angels
at the world's awakening

roads lead from open hands
lines and intersections
lizard interstices

our horses
are heavy
with unfulfilled direction
hands inquire at the sky's cheek
the sky bends down
hands touch the fabric of a single chord
the sky unfurls
into velvet dunes of rippling sound

50

Diplomacy

I met someone today
who mistook me for you.
she said we had so much to catch up on
you and she

but she didn't even say that
in so many words.
she said

that in the years intervening
between today and her leaving
the thought of dividing you somehow, of
waking up with you and leading
a speechless existence, dwelling
each day on the minute details of living
(you in her life and she in yours)

would creep into her mind at the oddest hours.
she said that she is afraid, her body
is too white, but that the fear
is a part of the beauty of that part of you
which she took away and would not return.
she said that words
should pass between you as music passes —
she mistook me entirely. to speak with her,

to attend
the delicate voices that clamour
at the surface of her skin, her face, hair,
her eyes, was like performing at an
ambassadorial dinner. I had no idea
what she meant. I said
you had gone away.
was it the right thing to say? if you love her
half as much as I want her now,

find her, enter her sleep.

52

Giant Fish
(*fragments of a lost chronicle*)

none of us knew better
than to go out in the rain
and meet them:
giant fish
rising from the sea

anticipate them with mechanical smiles
waiting on the glinting pebbles
rutted by the tide.

when two races meet
on the brink of their two kingdoms
questions are asked, as protocol demands,
to render conquest comprehensible
and they asked us in the shadow of our
separate worlds, had we too come
for a reason more than death
did we too strain toward a higher union
than body to like body could allow —

fish
sliding soundlessly over the breakwater.

'Turn back.' some of us were afraid
all of us lost that night
and the wind was gliding in the eaves
our granite walls tormented
by the water's cold approach
and our fires had sunk through moss.
we prayed: 'Turn back,
turn back giant fish: turn back
and lie on other bodies' but like fools

none of us knew better
than to gather at the dark border of
our shrinking world, not knowing why or
what could be achieved
but just to wait
just to see them first.

at that crux of our history
when everything among us had been said
every transaction completed
every song sung, every profit gained
and everything ultimately lost,
hundreds among us actually wanted
to proclaim truth
(there had never been so many

no, not since the beginning this
squealing roaring rabbling maze
of truth)

giant fish were shadows
rolling in the surf.

2.

apart from the water, which we can't breathe
what scares us is their love
intangibility and silence

54

we think they died in droves
before they brought us back
but they don't believe in martyrs
and we too think of our dead
less often now.

every day a little of our memory leaves us.
the old sequence of years
flows into a single night
ancient houses on scattered hills
dissolve in rain
naked men and women
wait on the shore
beyond the farthest wall
the farthest reach of space

we have old affinities
within these foggy globes
rejoin a prior passion
harden build design perfect
our age's end
drink the substance of their victory
until, frightened by the offer of their lives
we promise all to their indifference, swell
like toads within the skin of sanity

but all of us live while they are dying

who knows why we do anything.
time passes outside our knowledge
but we know that nothing ends

a clock marks the meeting
of our consecutive worlds
and we must travel through them all,
a ragged caravan.

3.

turn back
turn back giant fish
turn back solitary guardians
turn back turn back
go back and lie on
other bodies

we all have something to say
before we go
we all think we are proud
and don't need anything
turn back giant fish
turn back turn back

(giant fish give us everything
giant fish hang themselves on
high hooks and bleed into our mouths
we observe their silent passion
and their mysterious integration of the world
and they are in our bodies)

turn back giant fish
turn back turn back
turn back you deadly energy
turn back turn back
turn back you heatless agony
turn back   turn back

4.

you, in a distant reality
may grope back in your windswept mind
to your gentle beginning in an arid ruin
but must know nothing, even less than I
of what is past
who am the chronicler only of
tonight's short dream.
the earth contains your history
but you, choosing to forget,
hear only the wind
screaming in your high caves
and each day affords only
a single day's respite
and each night reaffirms
a blank eternity.

57

fool, merchant, creator of life within life
father, watcher of the sky
creator of teeming artifacts of terror
progenitor of warmth, carrier
of rich disease

in this fantasy we recognize your face
in the annihilation at dream's end we recognize
you
while the erupting blood of giant fish
sears red our sky
and we, devoid of lifelessness, disgorge our
lives
and flower briefly into meat.

58

Escape

before long, we were all
thinking about escape: someone
said there'd be a boat with jewelled oars,
water-spiders would dart
on two straight ripples from the bow.
every day, there were our faces,
time-eaten, peering down the wharf
with onyx eyes while the spiders lay still,
resting on the water as we did
on chances, possibilities.

then sometimes wars were fought
by the mammoth clouds, they ate
each other with jaws
tailored precisely to each other's sizes, shapes.
decisions were constantly made, and
one man always heard a sound like singing.
children captured unknown insects,
brought them home, where they
shrilled all night in a bottle.

59

why of course we'll all
get out of here someday, our expectant
dances make the stars brood,
now so many people lie around
wrapped in dreams, cradled
like relics in soft wool, as if
invisibly attended to; escape must have
come to them like the shards of a mirror,
but with hands that reached
and quietly drew them aside. I myself

had this dream last night:
a fish lay in the water like a silver arc,
like the moon playing at being a fish.
I shot an arrow into its side
and it leapt high, it was sunrise,
then it was a boat with glittering oars
and finally a bird which ate the sky
with one shriek. awake,
I am surrounded by those who remain.
their eyes are onyx
agate, amethyst

they touch me with words
with a whispered fugue.

Rondelay

you will continue to live every day

and the sun will rise
whether you sleep or stay up

the sun will set
indoors and out

and you will lose time
in the doorway shadows.

maybe love will come there

more beautiful and patient
than anyone

we will dress in coarse linen
and crushed lilacs will lie beneath us

where we lie

61

sing rondelay rondelay

every day
you will pass

and not see the shadows where we lie

rondelay rondelay
you will say

you have lost
the wonderful place where those two lie.

you will continue to live every day
and the sun will rise

oh you will greet
day by day

the merciless sun.

62

Contents